THE COARSE FISHING RECORD BOOK

Overview of the history of the sport

Throughout history, fishing has been one of the primary means of putting food on the table for your family. Before the invention of specific fishing gear, hunters typically ate whatever they caught. However, as technology improved, and gear developed, in the mid-nineteenth-century hunters searched for tastier fish, particularly those under the salmonid's category (e.g. salmon, trout etc). The gear necessary for this was different than before and required different knowledge and skills. It also meant this type of fishing, today called game fishing, became more popular with the English gentry as higher levels of wealth, and the transport revolution, meant they could go to places such as Scotland to ensure they caught the best salmon.

Freshwater fish outside of this group were seen as having the texture of needles or cotton wool thus undesirable, these fish became known as coarse fish, sometimes rough fish, to differentiate them from game fish. Coarse fishing then became a sport in and of itself. As time progressed, coarse fishing became more popular. By 1995, for example, there were 2.3 million anglers coarse fishing in England and Wales.

Introduction to Coarse Fishing

In the UK, it is estimated anglers spent some £1.46 billion in 2017 on tackle, bait, clothing, accommodation, petrol, permits etc. people go coarse fishing each year. For all anglers in England and Wales, anybody over the age of 12 must purchase a valid rod licence before fishing legally for coarse fish.

According to research conducted by the government, in England, freshwater angling contributes £1.46 billion to the economy, and supported 27,000 full-time equivalent jobs in 2015. There were also 19.4 million days spent coarse fishing in the same year, and carps were the most popular individual species. On average, anglers spend an average of £400 on tackle and £110 on club or syndicate fuel. Overall, fuel and bait accounts for the bulk of expenditure on specific trips though most coarse angling trips take place between 5 and 25 miles from the angler's home so you don't have to worry about going far!

Why go?

People choose to go coarse fishing for several different reasons, all equally valid. Some anglers go out purely for pleasure, to enjoy a relaxing day by the water and to see what fish they can catch. Others compete in matches, either as individuals or in teams and gather at a particular venue to see how many fish they can catch in a certain time period, or who can amass the greatest weight of fish. These competitions are held locally, nationally, and even internationally. Alternatively, some individuals go out with the aim of catching a large fish of a specific species, known as specimen hunting. This involves angling for one particular species.

Techniques: The Basics

There are several different techniques used when coarse fishing depending on the situation and the type of fish you are trying to tackle. The most common method is rod and reel (also known as the pole and whip).

Float fishing: There are many things to consider when float fishing – the type of float used, the bobber stop, the mainline, the weight of the float, a bead, duo-lock/snap, swivel, leader, and hook. In float fishing, the bait is suspended using a float made out of hollow wood, plastic, cork, foam, or quill. In order to spot the float, it is usually painted a bright colour such as orange so you can tell when the fish bites as it will cause the painted float to dip under the surface of the water. This will only happen if you have your float set up correctly, it should point straight up when it comes down the water channel, if the top of the float is angled towards the river, that means you're dragging along the bottom and need to change the length of it.

Lure fishing: Lure fishing, also known as spinning (depending on the item used) is when an angler uses something to attract the fish's attention, usually attached to the end of the fishing line. This may be via vibration, flash, colour, or movement. These lures are often equipped with hooks to help catch the fish when they strike on the item, particularly carnivorous fish such as perch, zander, and pike.

Legering/ Bottom fishing: Known in the UK as legering, (bottom fishing elsewhere), this style of fishing involves catching fish at the bottom of a body of a water. The idea is to put your bait at the bottom of the water to lure in the fish, particularly groundfish such as bream, crappie, and catfish that lurk at the bottom. Though it seems like an easy technique, it requires anchoring and drifting skills.

Types of water

A pond is the best environment for beginners. Of course, on the whole, they're relatively gentle/ still so it makes sure your tackle doesn't move about. It's also easier as you do not need to cast your line as far. A slow-moving stream, on the other hand, allows you to drop your float and let it drift with the current. The faster it is, the more challenging it is as the current tries to pull your bait in an arc under the bank and further downstream. Alternatively, you may fish on a lake, you will find similar fish to what is in a pond, but it is more challenging as you have to find the areas of the lake that fish are attracted to, it's good for those looking to improve their skills. Finally, rivers are the hardest of all (depending on their flow of course), as it can be hard to control your tackle, fish can be hiding anywhere, and rivers are constantly changing. On the plus side, you can also find more fish than in any of the previous bodies and with practice, it will grow easier. Remember to fact this into the planning you do for your next trip.

BARBEL

BARBUS BARBUS

Family: Cyprinidae
Length: 20-36 in (50-91 cm)
Weight: up to 10 lb (4.5 kg)
Life Span: 15-20 Years

A barbus barbus (known simply as the Barbel in Great Britain), of the Barbus species, is a small, freshwater fish similar to a carp and is a popular sport fish. In the UK, they are native to eastern-flowing rivers in England but have been historically translocated to western-flowing rivers such as the River Severn. They are relatively common fish and are in the category of 'least concern' when it comes to conservation status.

Regarding appearance, adult Barbel specimens can reach up to 36 in (91 cm) in length and 10 lb (4.5 kg) in weight, though they are usually smaller than this. Left alone, adult barbel can live over 20 years of age. Barbel's also have a slender body, sloped forehead, flattened underside, and are complete with horizontally-orientated pectoral fins to help maintain depth while swimming in fast-flowing, deep rivers. These fins ensure they can stay close to the riverbed. When it comes to colour, adults are usually bronze, grey, or dark brown with a pale underbody and orange/ reddish fins. Meanwhile, their younger offspring are typically gwrey and mottled in appearance.

To get food, Barbels often venture out during the night. The common Barbel typically eats benthic organisms such as insect larvae, molluscs, and crustaceans. They only usually feed during the day if they are in deeper water of if they are located close to underwater obstructions. As such, when searching for barbel's, you are most likely to find success in fast-flowing rivers that have stone or gravel bottoms. That said, if you are lucky you can also find them in slower rivers and even stillwaters, though this is not as common.

The common Barbel is actually particularly hard to catch as they are both strong and fast. Should you wish to catch one in the UK, there are a few preferred rivers to do so: Dorset Stour, Trent, Severn, Hampshire Avon, Great Ouse and the Wye. Different bait is used too depending on where you are. Popular bait includes fishmeal-based pellets, boilies, maggots, hemp seed, and tinned luncheon meats.

BREAM

ABRAMIS BRAMA

Family: Cyprinidae
Length: 13-21 in (30-55 cm)
Weight: up to 8 lb (4 kg)
Life Span: 15-20 years

The common bream, also known as a freshwater bream, bronze bream, carp bream, or simply bream, is a European freshwater fish in the Cyprinidae family. A common bream is in the category of least concern when it comes to conservation status and are typically found in nutrient-rich ponds, lakes, canals, and slow-flowing rivers, particularly those with muddy bottoms and plenty of algae to feed on.

Typically, bream live in schools near the bottom of their environment. At night, they may feed closer to the shore but can usually only be seen in the daytime if it is particularly clear water. They usually feed on water plants, plankton, tubifex worms, gastropods, chironomid larvae, and gastropods.

Bream fish are usually silver-grey, though can appear more bronze-coloured when they age. Further, Bream are usually between 13-21 in (30-55cm) long and weigh between 4-8 lb (2-4 kg). Feature wise, the common bream has a high-backed laterally flattened body with a slightly undershot mouth but are often mistaken for a silver or white bream, particularly when younger. To distinguish between the three, count the scales from the first ray of the dorsal fin to the lateral line. Common bream has 11 or over while silver bream has fewer than 10 rows.

The common bream is usually not caught for human consumption, rather they are more popular in sports. Typical bait used to catch a bream includes sweetcorn, maggots/ worms, or boilies. Once interested in the bait, they are relatively easy to bring to the surface as they are flat and disc-shaped, allowing for an easier catch.

CARP

CYPRINUS CARPIO

Family: Cyprinidae
Length: 9-31 in (5-80 cm)
Weight: up to 30 lbs (14 kg)
Life Span: 25-50 years

Native to Asia and later introduced to Europe and North America, a carp is a freshwater fish from the Cyprinidael family. There are several different fish under the name carp, but the most sighted one is a common carp. These are prized fish as they are particularly difficult to hook as they often live alone or in small schools.

They are considered vulnerable to extinction, most likely because they are often regarded as a destructive invasive species – seeking for food, they roil the water which, in turn, increases turbidity and damages plants and animals in the area. In fact, they are the list drawn up by the Global Invasive Species Specialist Group which deems them in the top 100 of the World's Worst Invasive Alien Species.

Speaking of habitat, although they can be found in most places, the common carp prefers large bodies of still or slow-moving water as well as vegetative sediments. They are omnivorous and though they often eat plants, they prefer to feast on insects, crawfish, benthic worms, and crustaceans. Typically, wild common carp are between 9-31 in (40-80 cm) in length but can grow up to 39 in (100 cm) in the right conditions. On average, the common carp weighs anywhere between 4-30 lb (2-14 kg).

The most popular bait to catch a carp in the UK is known as a boilie, this is made of a boiled paste comprised of eggs, milk proteins, and artificial flavours. However, using natural offerings and homemade dough baits are also frequently used.

CHUB

SQUALIUS CEPHALUS

Family: Cyprinidae
Length: 9-23 in (25–60 cm)
Weight: 3-6 lbs (1.5-3 kg)
Life Span: 14-20 years

Chub are shoaling fish, common in both North America and Europe. They are much more adaptable than most other species and will feed in cold conditions, when other fish are in a comatose state. In the UK they can be found in abundance in the Staffordshire and Worcestershire Canal and Shropshire Union Canal.

Being slow growers, chubs are a shoaling fish, with males reaching maturity in three to seven years and females four to eight. They are silver in colour with a greenish tint and can reach a size in length of up to 23 in (60 cm), weighing up to 6 lb (3 kg), living for up to 22 years in the wild.

The feeding habits of Chubs vary a great deal, as they are voracious feeders and will eat almost anything that drifts past them, including, shrimp, crustaceans, insects on the water surface, worms, even small fish and frogs. Therefore, you can use a multitude of baits to attract them.

The popular game fish enjoy cover so keep a look out for trees overhanging a deep pool of water along the riverside, as these are good examples of where to find them. As chub love oxygenated a water weir or spill way is another excellent place to spot them, especially in the warmer months.

DACE

LEUCISCUS LEUCISCUS

Family: Cyprinidae
Length: 3-11 in (10-25 cm)
Weight: 1-2 lb (0.5–1 kg)
Life Span: 8-16 years

The common dace, a member of the carp family, can be found in abundance, inhabiting tiny streams and large rivers of Northern Europe and Asia. It is a lively fish and can be identified by its small, silvery appearance, with slim rounded bodies and forked tail. They can easily be mistaken for tiny roaches, bleak or a baby chub as they are all similar. The main difference to tell them apart are their dorsal and anal fins that curve inwards.

Living up to 20 years, they average a weight of up to 2lb (1 kg) and grow to a length of between 3-11 in (10-25 cm). Spawning around April, the female deposits her yellow eggs at the roots of aquatic plants.

Dace feed mostly on insects and aquatic plant life, picking small molluscs from the river bed or flies that land on the surface. Due to their small mouths, simple baits are best used to catch dace, such as maggots, castors, hemp or bread baits.

Using a light float set up is the most popular way to catch them. Exclusively river dwellers, you will find shoals of dace living in clear, fast flowing, streams that are highly oxygenated. Keep a look out around weirs and pools, normally close to the surface.

IDE

LEUCISCUS IDUS

Family: Cyprinidae
Length: 8-16 in (22-43 cm)
Weight: 1-4 lb (0.5–1.8 kg)
Life Span: 10-15 years

Native to Europe and Asia, Ide are a common freshwater fish that can be found in various bodies of water such as rivers and ponds. Although native to Europe it was only introduced to Great Britain in 1874 as an ornamental fish and is now widespread. Popular species of Ide include Golden Orfe, Silver Orfe and the Blue Orfe

Having a typical cyprinid shape body, Ide are commonly silver in colour with pinkish red fins, although older fish bodies can turn yellow in colour. Fully matured Ides attain a length of 8-16 in (22-43 cm), and can weigh up to 4 lb (1.8 kg), although normal weight range is 0.5-3 lb (0.5–1.5 kg).

The fast-growing fish reaches sexual maturity at 3-5 years. Some populations will ascend rivers and streams where females will spawn in the shallow waters, laying their eggs on the gravelly or sandy bed. Females lay anywhere from 150,000 to 250,000 eggs, having a life span of 10-15 years.

Slow-flowing rivers, pools or still waters are the typical habitat for ide, leaving the shoreline for deeper waters as they grow bigger. Occurring in shoals, they prey on insects, larval, small mollusks and even small fish. Therefore, maggots and casters make the best bait.

PERCH

PERCA

Family: Percidae
Length: up to 15 in (40 cm)
Weight: up to 2 lb (1 kg)
Life Span: 7-12 years

The Genus Perca, commonly known as the Perch is a fish of the Percidae family, a species of fish found in fresh and brackish waters of the Northern Hemisphere. The European version can be found throughout Europe and Asia. With its spiky dorsal fin, the distinctive fish is one of the most colourful, characterised by its brown, yellow, orange tints, and tiger like stripes.

Living between 7-22 years the perch can reach a length of up to 15 in (40 cm) weighing up to 2 lb (1 kg) on average in the UK. Females spawn towards the end of April, beginning of May laying sticky bands of eggs amongst vegetation, or shrubs that are submerged, ready for the male to fertilise them.

They can be found across the UK in all types of water, lakes large and small rivers. As they are bottom feeders they are likely to be found lurking around large objects such as vegetation, undercut banks, tree roots and manmade structures.

With their large appetites, perch are not fussy eaters. Their normal diet is made up of insects, and crustaceans, with larger perch even eating small fish. Therefore, you can use many baits to catch them, however live bait such as maggots, insect lava even small minnows to be popular.

PIKE

ESOX LUCIUS

Family: Esocidae
Length: 22-23 in (55-85 cm)
Weight: up to 15 lb (6 kg)
Life Span: 10-25 years

The Northern pike takes its name from its resemblance to the, Late Middle Age, pole-like weapon. Its habitat can be found in brackish and fresh waters of the Northern Hemisphere, notably the United Kingdom, Ireland, the United States and most of Canada.

Pike have a distinct appearance, a large protruding snout with sharp teeth and long body, give the sign of a real predator. Olive green in colour, with a yellow to white shading on their belly, they can live for up to 15 years in the wild; average sized pike grow to length of between 22-35 in (55-85 cm), weighing up to 15 lb (6 kg).

Spring is the time when the species seek out shallow areas amongst weeds for spawning. Females lay their eggs on the stems of plant life. The eggs take on average between 10 to 1 days to hatch. Babies grow fairly quickly in the first few months, where both males and females will reach maturity in two to three years.

Pike are by nature carnivorous and will eat whatever they can swallow, normally other fish, including their own species, and have been even known to feed on frogs and ducks. They can be found in various different types of waters including ponds, rivers, streams and canals. The best bait for catching pike is dead bait, the fresher the better, although, ensure your tackle is strong.

ROACH

RUTILUS RUTILUS

Family: Cyprinidae
Length: 3-15 in (10-40 cm)
Weight: up to 2 lb (1 kg)
Life Span: 8-14 years

As one of the most widley distributed species of fish in the UK the roach, native to southern parts of England, is an extremely adaptable fish and has spread across many parts of the UK and is now, commonly, found around Europe, with the exception of an area around the Mediterranean.

Roach are a shoaling fish, with silver bodies and grey to orange fins, they can often be confused with rudd. An easy way to tell them apart is the by looking at the shape of the mouth, as the mouths of rudd are upturned.

Roach spawn from spring to early summer, in shallow waters close to the shore, when the water temperature is above 12°c. Females lay up to 100,000 tiny eggs that cling to plant life such as weeds. They are slow growers and may reach 3-15 in (10-40 cm) after 10 years, they generally adopt a life span of between 8-14 years.

A reason why roach are so successful is down to their ability to eat whatever they can find. During the warm weather you will find them feeding close to the surface, eating a wide range of foods, such as plant material, worms, maggots, with the young feeding on plankton. Therefore, some of the best baits to use include castors, maggots, pinkies, cheese and bloodworm.

RUDD

SCARDINIUS ERYTHROPHTHALMUS

Family: Cyprinidae
Length: 13-15 in (35-40 cm)
Weight: 2-5 lb (1-2 kg)
Life Span: 8 to 14 years

Rudd are a member of the carp family, they are commonly found throughout Europe and Central Asia. However, they are now considered an invasive species to countries where they have been artificially introduced into various countries, notably North America, as they have the potential to cause irreversible damage to indigenous ecosystems.

With similar characteristics to the roach it can be easily identified incorrectly. the brightly colouring of its fins can quickly give it away. Adopting a small head, with a bottom jaw protruding over the top it has a slim body which is a slick sheen of green and bronze colours.

During the spawning months a female can lay its, pale pink eggs of between one 100,00 to 200,000 per kg of bodyweight. An average sized rudd can grow up to 40 cm although adults can be as large as between 13-15 in (45-50 cm), weighing 2-5 lb (1-2 kg).

The summer, autumn months are best for catching rudd. Ideal locations are ponds, lakes and canals; still, clear, waters that are rich in plant life, since they tend to feed around weed beds and a diet of insects found around the surface. A range of bait can be used to entice them, anything from maggots, casters, sweetcorn and bread.

TENCH

TINCA TINCA

Family: Cyprinidae
Length: 15-27 in (40-70 cm)
Weight: 2-5 lbs (1-2 kg)
Life Span: 20-30 years

Perhaps one of the more attractive game fish, tench are considered a tough species that can survive in areas with very low oxygen levels. They can be predominately found in still water, whilst some can be found along lowland, slow moving, deep river systems.

With varying shades of green in colour, its features include a powerful rounded body with a large broad tail and is covered in a thick slime, making it rather difficult to hold. Although not proven, historically, it was referred to as the Doctor Fish. It was suggested that other fish would rub their bodies against them for their healing properties; this lead to the belief of boiling tench slime and using it as a medical treatment.

Compared to most other species tench require warmer water to spawn, around June -July. They have a slow growth rate and have a long lifespan of between 20-30 years. Small adults can grow to around 15 cm, weighing 3 lbs, where larger specimans can grow up to 28 inches (70 cm).

The best time to target tench can be made in the morning, when oxygen levels tend to be at their lowest and can be found not too far from weed beds, which provide cover and feeding areas. A give away sign are bubbles escaping from the gills, from when foraging and sifting debris in the weeds and silt. Their natural food include crustaceans and bloodworms. Therefore, red maggots and casters make a good bait, they also love hemp.

ZANDER

SANDER LUCIOPERCA

Family: Percidae
Length: 25-35 in (50-90 cm)
Weight: 6-8 lb (3-4 kg)
Life Span: 15-20 years

Zander are a member of the perch family, native to Eastern Europe where they are well known for being an appetizing dish. The zander was introduced to UK waterways in 1967, into the Great Ouse Relief Channel, located in Norfolk. Although, the species had been residing in ponds around in Britain for over 90 years prior. The fish are an aggressive predator and excel at hunting in murky waters.

Spawning between April to June, females can produce up to 200,000 eggs for each kilogram of their bodyweight. They are however slow growers and can typically grow between 25 to 35 in (50-90 cm) over six to eight years, weighing up to 8 lbs (4 kg). Greenish brown in appearance, they support a distinct long pointed snout with sharp Dracula like fangs, along with the spiny dorsal fin, it makes for a sinister appearance.

Starting out as vegetarian, they start preying on small fish when reaching adulthood. Smaller sized zander tend to hunt in packs. Therefore, deadbait, such as small dead roach, or better still, live bait is best used to catch zander.

The best place to fish for zander are the deepest, murky waters of canals and waterways churned up by boats. Look for features such as bridges or any locations where light levels are reduced so that they can hide. Due to the species being non-native it is technically illegal to return a zander back to British waters.

Date:

◯ ◯ ◯ ◯ ◯ ◯ ◯
M   T   W   T   F   S   S

Venue:

Start Time:

End Time:

Hours Fished:

Total Fish Caught:

Bait:

Notes:

Species	Length	Weight	Time

Species	Length	Weight	Time

Date:

M T W T F S S

Venue:

Start Time:

End Time:

Hours Fished:

Total Fish Caught:

Bait:

Notes:

Species	Length	Weight	Time

Species	Length	Weight	Time

Fishing Record

Date:

○ ○ ○ ○ ○ ○ ○
M T W T F S S

Venue:

Start Time:

End Time:

Hours Fished:

Total Fish Caught:

Bait:

Notes:

Species	Length	Weight	Time

Species	Length	Weight	Time

Date:

M T W T F S S

Venue:

Start Time:

End Time:

Hours Fished:

Total Fish Caught:

Bait:

Notes:

Species	Length	Weight	Time

Species	Length	Weight	Time

Date:

M T W T F S S

Venue:

Start Time:

End Time:

Hours Fished:

Total Fish Caught:

Bait:

Notes:

Species	Length	Weight	Time

Species	Length	Weight	Time

Date:

M T W T F S S

Venue:

Start Time:

End Time:

Hours Fished:

Total Fish Caught:

Bait:

Notes:

Species	Length	Weight	Time

Species	Length	Weight	Time

Fishing Record

Date:

○ ○ ○ ○ ○ ○ ○
M T W T F S S

Venue:

Start Time:

End Time:

Hours Fished:

Total Fish Caught:

Bait:

Notes:

Species	Length	Weight	Time

Species	Length	Weight	Time

Date:

○ ○ ○ ○ ○ ○ ○
M T W T F S S

Venue:

Start Time:

End Time:

Hours Fished:

Total Fish Caught:

Bait:

Notes:

Species	Length	Weight	Time

Species	Length	Weight	Time

Fishing Record

Date:

M T W T F S S

Venue:

Start Time:

End Time:

Hours Fished:

Total Fish Caught:

Bait:

Notes:

Species	Length	Weight	Time

Species	Length	Weight	Time

Date:

M T W T F S S

Venue:

Start Time:

End Time:

Hours Fished:

Total Fish Caught:

Bait:

Notes:

Species	Length	Weight	Time

Species	Length	Weight	Time

Fishing Record

Date:

◯ ◯ ◯ ◯ ◯ ◯ ◯
M T W T F S S

Venue:

Start Time:

End Time:

Hours Fished:

Total Fish Caught:

Bait:

Notes:

Species	Length	Weight	Time

Species	Length	Weight	Time

Date:

M T W T F S S

Venue:

Start Time:

End Time:

Hours Fished:

Total Fish Caught:

Bait:

Notes:

Species	Length	Weight	Time

Species	Length	Weight	Time

Date:

M T W T F S S

Venue:

Start Time:

End Time:

Hours Fished:

Total Fish Caught:

Bait:

Notes:

Species	Length	Weight	Time

Species	Length	Weight	Time

Fishing Record

Date:

◯ ◯ ◯ ◯ ◯ ◯ ◯
M T W T F S S

Venue:

Start Time:

End Time:

Hours Fished:

Total Fish Caught:

Bait:

Notes:

Species	Length	Weight	Time

Species	Length	Weight	Time

Fishing Record

Date:

○ ○ ○ ○ ○ ○ ○
M T W T F S S

Venue:

Start Time:

End Time:

Hours Fished:

Total Fish Caught:

Bait:

Notes:

Species	Length	Weight	Time

Species	Length	Weight	Time

Date:

M T W T F S S

Venue:

Start Time:

End Time:

Hours Fished:

Total Fish Caught:

Bait:

Notes:

Species	Length	Weight	Time

Species	Length	Weight	Time

Date:

M T W T F S S

Venue:

Start Time:

End Time:

Hours Fished:

Total Fish Caught:

Bait:

Notes:

Species	Length	Weight	Time

Species	Length	Weight	Time

Fishing Record

Date:

M   T   W   T   F   S   S

Venue:

Start Time:

End Time:

Hours Fished:

Total Fish Caught:

Bait:

Notes:

Species   Length   Weight   Time

Species	Length	Weight	Time

Date:

○ ○ ○ ○ ○ ○ ○
M   T   W   T   F   S   S

Venue:

Start Time:

End Time:

Hours Fished:

Total Fish Caught:

Bait:

Notes:

Species	Length	Weight	Time

Species	Length	Weight	Time

Date:

M T W T F S S

Venue:

Start Time:

End Time:

Hours Fished:

Total Fish Caught:

Bait:

Notes:

Species	Length	Weight	Time

Species	Length	Weight	Time

Date:

M T W T F S S

Venue:

Start Time:

End Time:

Hours Fished:

Total Fish Caught:

Bait:

Notes:

Species	Length	Weight	Time

Species	Length	Weight	Time

Date:

M T W T F S S

Venue:

Start Time:

End Time:

Hours Fished:

Total Fish Caught:

Bait:

Notes:

Species	Length	Weight	Time

Species	Length	Weight	Time

Date:

M T W T F S S

Venue:

Start Time:

End Time:

Hours Fished:

Total Fish Caught:

Bait:

Notes:

Species	Length	Weight	Time

Species	Length	Weight	Time

Date:

M T W T F S S

Venue:

Start Time:

End Time:

Hours Fished:

Total Fish Caught:

Bait:

Notes:

Species	Length	Weight	Time

Species	Length	Weight	Time

Date:

○ ○ ○ ○ ○ ○ ○
M T W T F S S

Venue:

Start Time:

End Time:

Hours Fished:

Total Fish Caught:

Bait:

Notes:

Species	Length	Weight	Time

Species	Length	Weight	Time

Fishing Record

Date:

◯ ◯ ◯ ◯ ◯ ◯ ◯
M T W T F S S

Venue:

Start Time:

End Time:

Hours Fished:

Total Fish Caught:

Bait:

Notes:

Species	Length	Weight	Time

Species	Length	Weight	Time

Date:

M T W T F S S

Venue:

Start Time:

End Time:

Hours Fished:

Total Fish Caught:

Bait:

Notes:

Species	Length	Weight	Time

Species	Length	Weight	Time

Date:

M T W T F S S

Venue:

Start Time:

End Time:

Hours Fished:

Total Fish Caught:

Bait:

Notes:

Species	Length	Weight	Time

Species	Length	Weight	Time

Date:

○ ○ ○ ○ ○ ○ ○
M T W T F S S

Venue:

Start Time:

End Time:

Hours Fished:

Total Fish Caught:

Bait:

Notes:

Species	Length	Weight	Time

Species	Length	Weight	Time

Fishing Record
Date:
M   T   W   T   F   S   S
Venue:
Start Time:
End Time:
Hours Fished:
Total Fish Caught:
Bait:
Notes:
Species   Length   Weight   Time

Species	Length	Weight	Time